Contents

CW01664648

Introduction

General and scope

1 This JCT Tendering Practice Note 2017 is a revised edition of the previous 2012 edition. (The 2012 edition was based on the original JCT Practice Note 6, published in 2002 as a successor to the NJCC Codes of Procedure for selective tendering.)

2 This Practice Note is intended for use by both the public and private sectors. In relation to the public sector, it indicates some of the key areas where EU public procurement rules impact on aspects of tendering procedure. The principal changes in the present edition are to reflect revisions made to those rules. The present edition is also intended to reflect developments there have been in best practice relevant to both sectors.

3 This Practice Note consists of:

- a general commentary on tendering practices and procedures, focusing on selective single stage, two stage and competitive dialogue tendering procedures; and
- Model Forms compiled by the JCT included in Appendix A and Appendix B to this Note.

4 Unless it is clear from its context that reference to public sector procurement is intended, any commentary on any aspect of tendering in this Practice Note should be understood as applying to private sector procurement only. The Model Forms in the Appendices are relevant solely to private sector procurement.

Public sector procurement – legal framework

5 Public sector procurement is subject to a legal framework of EU rules that are revised from time to time and are implemented in national legislation in Member States. The UK rules are at present contained in The Public Contracts Regulations 2015 ('the PC Regulations'). These regulations implemented EU Public Contracts Directive 2014/24/EU and entered into force in England, Wales and Northern Ireland on 26th February 2015[1][2]. Subject to certain transitional provisions, the regulations replaced their predecessor, the 2006 Public Contracts Regulations.

6 The PC Regulations apply where the Employer is a 'contracting authority' and the contract being awarded a 'public contract' as defined in the regulations. The regulations apply when the contract being awarded is within the scope of the regulations and exceeds a value threshold.[3] The JCT recommends appropriate legal advice is taken if there is any doubt as to the applicability of the regulations.

7 This Practice Note does not aim to cover every aspect of the PC Regulations and is not a guide to them. For public sector procurements where the PC Regulations apply, Employers and their consultants must have regard to the requirements of the regulations including any guidance issued by GOV.UK, and seek specialist advice whenever necessary. For further guidance on the PC Regulations and other legislation applicable to public procurement please refer to www.gov.uk/guidance/public-sector-procurement-policy.

Model Forms and their use

8 As indicated above, the Model Forms are only intended for use in relation to private sector procurements. The forms cover both the pre-selection phase and the tendering stage, and are largely unchanged in this edition. The forms are designed to be used as templates and as a useful point of reference, and will require adapting for use in relation to individual projects. They may be used with any JCT main contract form and with necessary adaptations, may also be used for sub-contract and framework tendering and with other construction contracts.[4] With regard to the public sector, in view of the rules and regulations that apply to public procurement referred to above, public sector Employers and their professional advisers will usually have developed their own forms for use in the

---

[1] There are separate regulations in Scotland, namely the Public Contracts (Scotland) Regulations 2015.

[2] The Public Procurement (Amendments, Repeals and Revocations) Regulations 2016 update various pieces of legislation including the PC Regulations and should be read together with the PC Regulations.

[3] Where a contract value falls below the relevant threshold, the regulations may still have some application; for further guidance please refer to www.gov.uk/guidance/public-sector-procurement-policy.

[4] It is to be noted that in the case of sub-contract and framework tendering the same good practice principles should apply as for main contracts.

tendering process. For this reason, the JCT has not considered it appropriate to include model forms in this Note suitable for use by the public sector.

9 In this edition, the Model Form of Pre-Qualification Questionnaire (Appendix A.3) is unchanged and remains in checklist form. Employers and/or their professional advisers will in many cases have developed their own preferred format for the necessary questions. In the case of public sector works with contract values that are above the EU threshold and subject to the PC Regulations, guidance has been issued by the Crown Commercial Service (CCS) in relation to the use and content of pre-qualification questionnaires that Employers must have regard to (r107 of the PC Regulations). Under the CCS's current guidance, Employers may use the PAS 91 question sets[5] or the latest version of the Standard Questionnaire (the Standard Questionnaire is a document produced in guidance issued by the CCS that includes a set of standard selection questions). Alternatively, tendering contractors may use the European Single Procurement Document[6]. JCT recommends that for up to date information on guidance issued including the latest version of the Standard Questionnaire, the parties refer to GOV.UK.

Selective Tendering Procedures

10 This Practice Note is essentially concerned with selective single-stage, two-stage and competitive dialogue tendering procedures[7] under which, in order to be included in the shortlist of those selected to bid, interested contractors are required to pre-qualify through responses to a Pre-Qualification Questionnaire or Standard Questionnaire. For public sector works with contract values that are above the EU threshold and subject to the PC Regulations, the selection process is normally required to be preceded by issuing a notice on both Contracts Finder[8] and in the Official Journal of the European Union (OJEU)[9].

11 Single-stage selective tendering is primarily appropriate where the Employer's requirements are sufficiently defined to enable the work to be priced. Two-stage and competitive dialogue procedures are generally reserved for complex projects where the Employer's requirements have not crystallised and contractor/specialist input is required for the purpose (although for completeness it should be remembered that, under the public sector procurement rules, restricted procedures, although involving a distinct short-listing stage, must not involve negotiation during the second, tender stage).

12 The criteria for the initial selection assessment, which should be established before expressions of interest are invited (or, in public sector procurement, before the OJEU notice), should be objective, fair, transparent and non-discriminatory. Apart from matters of good standing and compliance on the part of the tendering body, its directors and officers, those criteria should generally be limited to matters of appropriate financial strength, technical capability, record and resources to carry out the project successfully.

13 In single and two-stage tendering, shortlisting is followed by the tender process, at the end of which, in a single-stage procedure, the successful tenderer is awarded the contract. In two-stage tendering, the successful bidder is selected as preferred bidder, to assist the Employer and professional team in finalising the design in the pre-construction stage and then to negotiate the final terms of the contract.

14 Under the competitive dialogue procedure, the shortlist comprises those selected for a dialogue with the Employer and the professional team to help develop the best solution for the project.

15 For public sector procurements where the PC Regulations apply and which involve negotiation, the number of tenderers selected for the dialogue must generally be 3 or more and, while the dialogue itself can be divided into stages, the number involved at each stage must remain sufficient to ensure competition. When the Employer identifies one or more acceptable solutions, the dialogue ends and tenders are called for from each member of the

---

[5] PAS 91 is a standardised pre-qualification questionnaire developed by the British Standards Institution (BSI). PAS 91 was last updated in 2013 and is currently being revised to reflect current legislation, including the 2015 CDM Regulations.

[6] Under regulation 59 of the PC Regulations, in relation to the submission of requests to participate in the tendering process or of tenders, contracting authorities are required to accept the European Single Procurement Document.

[7] It should be noted that the categories of procedure listed here and elsewhere in this note are not intended to reflect the procedures used in the public sector, where the term "single stage tendering" would generally apply to an "open procedure", in which interested contractors may submit a tender in response to a contract notice and the tenders are then evaluated to establish a preferred bidder(s). Shortlisting will not form part of the process. A "restricted procedure" has pre-qualification and tendering as separate stages, but involves no negotiation. The two multi-stage procedures involving negotiation are called "competitive procedure with negotiation" and "competitive dialogue". There are other procedures not described in this note and a full description of any public sector procedure is outside the scope of this note.

[8] This is a web based portal provided by or on behalf of the Cabinet Office.

[9] The PC Regulations include some provisions that apply to below threshold contracts. These include the requirement for contracting authorities to publish information about a contract opportunity on Contracts Finder within 24 hours of the time when they first advertise the opportunity in any other way (r110).

shortlist. (Under the PC Regulations, those tenders must be judged on a 'most economically advantageous' basis, rather than lowest price.)

Two-stage tendering

16 As indicated, two-stage tendering has advantages in complex projects where the Employer's requirements are not settled: it increases the scope for value engineering, through early contractor involvement, team work and fixed (rather than estimated) sub-contractor pricing, and it reduces the scope for claims that result from inaccurate or inadequate designs or specification. With the design and procurement processes being in part concurrent, it may also save time.

17 The first stage of the two-stage process involves competitive tenders, but that is often inevitably restricted to preliminaries, overheads, contractor's profit and those elements of the design that are sufficiently advanced to allow proper pricing. If, as traditionally tended to be the case, there then remains a need to agree the Contractor's final price, that is viewed by public procurement authorities as a negotiated procedure, permissible only in exceptional circumstances.

Two-stage tendering and public procurement – special considerations

18 In a public procurement two stage process, the Contractor completes a Pre-Qualification Questionnaire or Standard Questionnaire as part of the first stage[10]. The questionnaire will contain questions that relate to the Contractor's organisation and the mandatory and selection criteria. The responses to the questionnaire are then evaluated and a shortlist is created. The Contractors on the shortlist are then invited to tender (Invitation to Tender). The second stage of the process after shortlisting normally comprises scored award questions (i.e. on how the works are going to be carried out) and the obtaining of information on pricing elements and possibly also implementation/project plans. The Invitations to Tender are assessed and a preferred bidder identified.

19 Regulation 53 of the PC Regulations requires contracting authorities, by electronic means, to offer full and unrestricted access to the 'procurement documents' from the date that a contract notice is published in the OJEU. The term procurement documents is defined in the regulations and will include questionnaires, technical specifications and the proposed conditions of contract. The JCT understands that following implementation of the PC Regulations it is now common practice in the public sector to issue a "draft" Invitation to Tender with the Pre-Qualification Questionnaire/Standard Questionnaire for information purposes.

Practice and use across the United Kingdom

20 Tendering practice appears to be generally uniform across England and Wales and JCT is not aware of material differences between that and practice in Northern Ireland. However, where a JCT Contract is to be governed by Northern Ireland law, it should incorporate necessary adaptations such as those included in the Northern Ireland Adaptation Schedules, published by the Royal Society of Ulster Architects.

21 Scottish law and practice differ in certain respects from law and practice in the remainder of the United Kingdom and, in terms of forms used in the tendering process, practice has historically appeared more diverse in Scotland than elsewhere. However, it is intended that this Practice Note and its forms should also serve as a general guide in cases governed by Scottish law where a Scottish Building Contract Committee (SBCC) version of a JCT Contract is to be used.

22 UK government policy and support for a standard, simplified approach to accreditation and pre-qualification procedures, together with the public sector procurement regime, the growth of electronic tendering and joint purchasing arrangements have over the last decade contributed and will no doubt continue to contribute to the standardisation process.

23 The UK Government as a customer, through implementation of its 2011 Government Construction Strategy and in seeking to drive down both procurement and whole-life costs, continues to try out various alternative forms of procurement and contractual arrangements, aimed at early contractor involvement and teamwork.[11]

---

[10] See the commentary above on questionnaires for use in public sector procurement and on the different procedures.

[11] See also the 2016 - 20 Government Construction Strategy (www.gov.uk).

The Preliminary Enquiry

The documents – Model Forms

24 After preparation of an initial list of potential contractors, and to establish which are best suited to the project and willing to bid, each contractor should be sent an Enquiry Letter. A Model Form for use in preparation of an Enquiry Letter is included in Appendix A (A.1). The letter should be accompanied by a document setting out the relevant project information (a Project Information Schedule) and a Pre-Qualification Questionnaire. A Model Form of Information Schedule and a checklist for the Questionnaire are also set out in Appendix A (A.2 and A.3)[12]. Again, it should be remembered that the Model Forms in the Appendices relate to private sector procurements.

Time for responses

25 In terms of the minimum period for responses to pre-qualification questionnaires, the period in the case of public sector procurement above the relevant threshold is generally 30 days from date of the dispatch of the OJEU notice, subject to certain exceptions; it reduces to 15 days in urgent cases which meet set criteria. Broadly speaking, comparable timescales apply to tender responses, but there is variation between the different procedures. It is to be noted there is no set period for tender responses in competitive dialogue. In the case of private sector procurements, the period may be substantially less – for single-stage tendering where Contractor's design is not required and the questionnaire is straightforward, 14 or 21 days may be adequate. However, a longer period will be appropriate for cases involving such design, or if the questionnaire or required responses are substantially more detailed or the process coincides with a holiday period.

The Project Information Schedule

26 To encourage a positive response from as many of the prospective contractors as possible, it is important that the Project Information Schedule should be duly completed. It must provide contractors with information sufficient to enable them to decide whether or not to tender and should include details of:

- the project and its estimated value
- the Employer, the professional team and contact point
- the tendering procedure to be used (single-stage, two-stage or competitive dialogue) and the medium (electronic or hard copy)
- the programme, including anticipated dates for pre-selection interviews, issue of tender documents and tender submission
- the requirements for Contractor's design[13]
- any applicable BIM requirements[14]
- the Contract to be used
- completed Contract Particulars (or their equivalent), showing the requirements (or likely requirements) for Collateral Warranties or Third Party Rights, bonds and Contractor's insurances (including Professional Indemnity insurance, where there is Contractor's design work)
- any amendments or modifications of the Contract or its conditions

---

[12] To assist in the preparation of tender documents, users may wish also to consult BSI's BS 8534 ('Construction procurement policies, strategies and procedures – Code of practice (2011)'). It gives recommendations and guidance on the development of policies, strategies and procedures for the procurement of construction in the built environment. The standard applies to public or private sector client organisations. For information on BS8534 go to constructingexcellence.org.uk/bs8534.

[13] It is important, particularly in cases where there is any intended novation of the Employer's design team, that the Project Information Schedule should indicate clearly the design team's duties in respect of completion of the design and also those areas where input will be needed from specialist sub-contractors.

[14] A new version of BSI's Code of Practice governing collaborative production of architectural, engineering and construction information (BS1192) was published in 2016 (BS1192:2007+A2:2016).

- any requirements for parent company guarantees or for performance or other bonds that are not covered by the Contract Particulars

- mode of execution (as a deed or as a simple contract)

- (if not specified in the Enquiry Letter) the basis and criteria for pre-selection, including weightings or order of importance

- the basis of contract award (lowest price or price and quality)

- where award is to be based on price and quality (i.e. the 'best value' or 'most economically advantageous' tender) and where established prior to issue of the Invitation (or public notice), a list or general statement of the quality criteria and the relative weightings that will be applied to each of those criteria and to price[15]

- in relation to errors in priced tender documents (in a private sector procurement) whether Alternative 1 or Alternative 2 will apply[16].

The Questionnaire

27 The purpose of the Questionnaire is to establish the suitability of prospective tenderers based on their record and technical capacity, with the aim also of making the subsequent assessment of tenders as straightforward as possible. Technical record and capacity will of course remain central to the assessment of best value tenders, but as will be seen from BS 8534, there is a distinction between the general factual nature of the pre-qualification questionnaire and the applied, forward-looking criteria to be used in assessing tender proposals.

28 The information sought by the Questionnaire should be limited to matters that are directly relevant or useful. It will generally divide into four main categories: first, the basic factual particulars; second, those questions (principally relating to financial matters and good standing) where serious convictions[17] or manifestly inadequate resources will automatically disqualify; third, other regulatory and compliance matters, where odd lapses occur even in well-run organisations and where the potential for corrective action means there must be a discretionary element in the pass/fail decision; fourth, matters of technical capacity – capabilities, skills and past performance – which require to be scored.

29 It is important that a consistent standard be applied in decisions not to select on grounds within the second or third categories mentioned. In relation to technical capacity criteria, BS 8534 suggests a weighting for each of the chosen criteria in scoring contractors against an overall technical capacity threshold. Proper notes and records of assessments should be kept so that those not selected to tender may be properly debriefed.

30 The scoring model and arrangements for the pre-selection assessment should be established in advance of the issue of Preliminary Enquiries or any related advertisement/notice. To minimise the likelihood of perverse results, the model should be tested, particularly if previously established weightings or criteria have been adjusted. The interview may form an important part of the evaluation process; it cannot itself form a discrete selection criterion but within the evaluation may be given appropriate weight. The process must nevertheless be transparent with equal treatment afforded to each prospective tenderer.

31 If any unusual criteria that fall outside the normal range of good standing, financial resources and technical ability are to be applied in the pre-selection process, attention should be drawn to them in the preliminary documents.

32 To ensure that the pre-selection process is readily manageable for all parties, it is suggested that:

- so far as practicable, prospective contractors should not be required to supply details that have been covered in obtaining their existing accreditations

- information that is clearly not required until the tender stage should be left until then

- there should be word limits on responses, proportionate to the importance of the question.

---

[15] Where the Employer's requirements are not finally settled (e.g. in competitive dialogue tendering), a definitive statement of criteria and weightings may be left to the Invitation to Tender. Where precise weightings have not been fixed, an indicative range or descending order of importance may be helpful at the pre-selection stage.

[16] See the **Assessment and award** section below.

[17] For further commentary on bribery and corruption etc., see the next section.

If further detail is needed, that can be dealt with by a supplemental request or at the preliminary interview.

33 In terms of the information supplied, JCT would stress the importance of taking up references on past projects and, when a contractor's tender is likely to be selected, carrying out appropriate 'reality checks' at that contractor's premises.

34 With regard to questionnaires for use in relation to public sector works with contract values that are above the EU threshold and subject to the PC Regulations, please see the commentary above in the Introduction.

Number of Tenderers and debriefing

35 Even with standardised accreditation and pre-qualification procedures and the use of electronic tender systems, tender preparation can be costly for all but the simplest of projects. It is important that the number of contractors selected to tender is strictly limited; abortive costs of preparing and evaluating tenders are an overhead cost and an inefficiency that ultimately is carried by the industry.

36 Each project or contract needs to be considered in context, but generally between 3 and 6 tenders should be sufficient. For a design and build scheme no more than 4 tenderers should be selected. It should be noted that the minimum numbers for public sector procurements involving an element of short-listing are 3 for procedures involving negotiation (see paragraph 15 above) and 5 for restricted procedures.

37 The appropriate number of tenders for framework contracts will vary depending on value and nature of the framework.

38 Contractors who have not been selected to go forward to the tendering stage should always be promptly informed and, on request, provided with appropriately detailed feedback. It is helpful to be able to demonstrate objective assessment of suitability through the ready availability of the scoring matrix for each candidate and the notes on which assessments were based. In public sector procurement cases, the regulations only provide for debriefing at the award stage[16], but it is clearly good practice – and in the interest of all parties – that feedback should be given to unsuccessful applicants at this earlier stage.

The Invitation to Tender and Tender

The documents

39 After a shortlist of tenderers has been drawn up (or, in the case of a competitive dialogue procedure, once the final stage of the competitive dialogue has been completed), then, as soon as the other tender documents are available for release (i.e. drawings and bills of quantities, specification or work schedules, together with the Employer's Requirements), the document packs should be issued or made available to tenderers with an Invitation to Tender and Tender Form (Model Forms of Invitation to Tender and Tender Form are at Appendix B).[18]

40 Separate Tender Forms should be provided for each alternative offer sought and each Tender Form should identify clearly the particular offer to which it relates.

41 Where tendering is in hard copy form, it remains good practice to send the documents in duplicate to each contractor, accompanied by separate envelopes, each with an appropriate identifier, both for each offer that is sought and also for the priced and other documents that are to accompany the tender. (The envelopes should not show the tenderer's name.)

Bribery and corruption etc.

42 Prior to commencement of the tender process, consideration should be given by Employers and their professional advisers to the management of procurement fraud risk and appropriate provisions included in the tender documents. Employers and their consultants will be likely to have established procedures for managing these risks and to have reflected these in their standard tender documentation. Provisions typically included allow for the removal of a contractor from the tender process for bribery, corruption, fraud, money laundering or conspiracy (such provisions may include a requirement for a certificate or undertaking from the Contractor that they have not been charged with any relevant offences) and may deal with competition law infringements and collusive tendering forms of behaviour.

43 The PC Regulations set out mandatory and discretionary grounds for excluding tenderers from taking part in a public procurement procedure that is subject to the regulations. Where these provisions apply to a public contract they should be reflected in the pre-qualification documents. Mandatory grounds for exclusion under the regulations include offences such as bribery and money laundering and discretionary grounds include other types of improper conduct that may trigger the possibility of an exclusion, such as certain types of serious professional misconduct. It is to be noted that in the 2015 regulations the list of mandatory and discretionary exclusion grounds set out in the 2006 regulations was widened.

Tendering periods

44 In the case of straightforward, single-stage tenders in the private sector that involve no material element of Contractor's design, the recommended period for the preparation and return of tenders would be a minimum of 28 days. In cases subject to the PC Regulations, the minimum period required by the regulations may be up to 35 days.

45 In the case of Design and Build contracts and contracts where there is a material Contractor's Designed Portion, the appropriate period will depend on the nature and complexity of the Employer's Requirements and the extent to which the design is prescribed or has been developed by the Employer. Where the design is not prescribed and has not been developed, a period of 3 to 4 months should be allowed but a longer period may be required where, for example, the project involves extensive specialist work and/or there are possible planning difficulties. On the other hand, where the Employer's Requirements contain detailed designs covering a substantial part of the works, a shorter period may be sufficient.

Quality Criteria

46 In cases governed by public sector procurement rules, the assessment of best value tenders must be based on recognised best value criteria, i.e. quality, price, technical merit, aesthetic, functional and environmental characteristics, running costs, cost effectiveness, lifecycle costs (including maintenance and technical assistance arrangements) and (where applicable) the period required for completion.

47 In cases where tendering is on a best value basis, the criteria and their respective weightings relative to price (including those attaching to any sub-criteria) must be set out, identified or confirmed in the Invitation to Tender.

---

[18] As to the Model Forms, please see the Introduction and footnote [21].

48 Where tenders are not to be assessed on wider best value criteria but allow the Contractor to specify a period or periods for mobilisation, for preliminary design work and/or for the construction work, time is a criterion and should be weighted, specified and scored against price in the normal way.

Documents to be supplied by the Contractor

49 In the case of contracts involving Contractor's design or where he is otherwise required to prepare and supply any other documents with his tender, details of those documents must be given in the Invitation to Tender and they should also be listed in the Tender Form.

50 In addition the Employer or his designated consultant should specify clearly the type and extent or level of the design work, drawings, specifications or other information required with tenders, the size and format in which they are to be prepared and, if they are to be sent separately from the tender, the time for and method of transmission.

Completing the forms

51 In completing the Invitation to Tender, the Employer or a designated consultant should indicate:

- the documents included with it
- the latest time and date for the return of tenders, together with the relevant address or transmission instructions[19]
- the contact point for communications, queries, document inspection and site visits
- the basis of award and, in best value cases, the criteria and weightings to be applied
- the arrangements and procedure selected for priced documents
- the documents to be supplied by the tendering contractor (e.g. Contractor's Proposals, designs, drawings, specifications, etc).

52 The Invitation to Tender or an accompanying document should also give tenderers any required information not previously supplied, together with a note of any changes in information previously supplied.

53 The Employer or his designated consultant should also complete the relevant parts of the Tender Form. With reference to the Model Form in Appendix B these include:

- the description and location of the works
- the name and address of the Employer
- the name and address of the tendering contractor
- relevant adjustments to the list of documents supplied by the Employer
- documents to be supplied by the tendering contractor
- particulars of the parent company guarantor (where required)
- the arrangements and procedure for priced documents
- the dates or periods for the commencement and (where set) completion of the works.

54 The latest time and date for submission of bids should be stated in the Tender Form as well as in the Invitation to Tender.

55 If arrangements are to be made for mid-tender interviews and site visits, this should be mentioned in the Invitation to Tender. Mid-tender interviews and site visits can benefit the Employer and the tenderer although may be more appropriate on large or more sophisticated projects.

---

[19] For single-stage selective tenders, the PC Regulations contain complex provisions regarding the minimum period for tender submission (up to 35 days), as well as those for the initial selection.

Tender Submission

56 Tenderers should complete the Tender Form or (where alternative tenders are requested) the Forms required and submit them in accordance with the instructions or, where sent in hard copy, return them in due time in the envelope(s) provided. Where priced or other documents are required to be submitted at the same time, these in hard copy cases should accompany the tender in their separate envelopes. (Electronic tendering systems do not generally allow for an equivalent arrangement.) The period for tendering may be extended, as is stated in the Invitation to Tender, but tenders received out of time should not be considered.

Tender Compliance

57 To ensure fair competitive tendering, it is essential that the tenders submitted are based on identical documents and are compliant with them, with no attempt to vary that basis through qualifications in the tenders.

58 If a tenderer considers that any of the tender documents or requirements are deficient or require clarification, whether technically or in contractual terms, he should inform the Employer or the Employer's designated consultant as soon as possible, preferably not less than 10 working days before the closing date for tenders.

59 If it is decided to amend or provide clarification of any of the documents, the Employer or his designated consultant should notify all tenderers at the same time and, if necessary, extend the period for tendering.

60 A tenderer who submits a qualified tender should be given an opportunity to withdraw the qualifications so as to produce a compliant tender, but without amending the price. If the tenderer refuses to withdraw the qualifications, the tender may need to be rejected.

Withdrawal and Lapse of Tenders

61 As a matter of good practice, a tender should not be withdrawn during the period for which it is expressed to remain open for acceptance, save under Alternative 1 in the circumstances mentioned below. Under English law, the traditional view is that the general right to withdraw an offer at any time before acceptance would be ousted only if, for example, the tender was executed as a deed or there was consideration from the Employer for the implied promise not to withdraw it – though there are circumstances in which such consideration might be inferred. Under Scottish law, however, an undertaking to keep an offer open for a definite period is binding and the offer cannot be recalled within that time.

62 In each case an offer will lapse if not accepted within the specified period. If no period for acceptance is specified, the offer (unless permissibly withdrawn or recalled) will remain open for a reasonable period. That, however, gives rise to uncertainty and a period for acceptance should always be stated.

Assessment and award

Assessment on criteria other than price

63 Where tenders are to be assessed on a best value basis rather than lowest price, the evaluation of tenders against non-price criteria should be completed independently of the examination of the priced documents. For tenders regulated by the public sector procurement rules, an assessment should be conducted on a best value basis, but an Employer will have some latitude to use price as a factor in assessing best value.

64 Where criteria have been established, the Employer must abide by them and by any particular weighting or order of importance attributed to them in the relevant documents. To do otherwise would leave the Employer and his advisers open to challenge by unsuccessful tenderers.

65 In parallel with any such assessment and the examination of priced documents, any Contractor's Proposals, designs, drawings and other documents submitted with tenders should be checked for consistency with the Employer's Requirements or other documents supplied by the Employer to which they relate. Similarly there is considerable value in post-tender interviews and any reality checks considered necessary or desirable should also be made.

Examination of Priced Documents and Errors

66 Priced documents should also be examined before a tender is recommended or accepted in order to detect any computational errors but good practice demands that a contractor's tendered prices should not be altered without justification. Where an examination of the priced documents reveals an error or discrepancy between these prices and the overall tender figure, there are several methods of dealing with the situation. With regard to the public sector, in view of the rules and regulations that apply to public procurement referred to in the Introduction, public sector Employers will have developed their own procedures and the comments that follow do not apply to the public sector. In the case of private sector procurement, JCT recommends use of one of the two procedures set out below. Under the first (Alternative 1), correction of the overall tender price is not permitted; under the second (Alternative 2), it is permitted.

67 The choice of Alternative must be made before contractors are invited to tender and should be reflected by the appropriate deletion, both in the Project Information Schedule and in the Invitation to Tender.

68 Alternative 1 may be inconsistent with a partnering approach and is not considered appropriate in two-stage tendering procedures. However, Alternative 2 is open to abuse if not properly supervised.

69 The examination of the priced documents supporting the tender under consideration should be made by the Employer and/or his consultant(s), each of whom should treat the documents as confidential. Details of the tenderer's pricing should not be disclosed to any other person.

70 If errors are discovered by the Employer's consultant, they should be reported to the Employer and steps taken to implement the applicable Alternative.

The Alternative Provisions

Alternative 1

71 The tenderer should be given details of the errors and afforded an opportunity of confirming or withdrawing his tender. If the tender is withdrawn, the priced documents of the next lowest or next best value tenderer should be examined; if there are errors or discrepancies in them, this tenderer also (and any subsequent tenderer in turn) should be given a similar opportunity to confirm or withdraw.

72 Where the tenderer confirms his tender, an endorsement should be added to the priced documents prior to acceptance, indicating that all rates or prices in those documents (excluding preliminary items, contingencies, prime cost sums and provisional sums) are to be considered as reduced or increased in the same proportion as the corrected total of priced items exceeds or falls short of his offer price (again excluding the items, contingencies and sums mentioned above). The endorsement should be signed by both parties.

Alternative 2

73 The tenderer should be given an opportunity of confirming his offer or of amending it to correct genuine errors. Should he elect to amend his offer with the result that the revised tender is no longer the lowest or best value tender, the offer that becomes the lowest or best value should be examined.

74 If the tenderer elects not to amend his offer, an endorsement will be required as in Alternative 1. If the tenderer does amend his tender figure, and possibly certain of the rates in his documents, he should either be allowed access to his original tender to insert and initial the correct details or be required to confirm all the alterations in a letter. If in the latter case his revised tender is then recommended for acceptance, a copy of the letter should be attached to the tender acceptance letter or form before that acceptance is sent or communicated in any way to the tenderer; the acceptance letter or form itself should record clearly that the amended tender figure and rates in the tenderer's letter are substituted for those in the original tender.

Post-tender discussions

75 As is well recognised, the involvement of the prospective contractor, the utilisation of his knowledge and experience and a full exchange of ideas in the development of the final design are obviously highly desirable and there are many single stage projects where gaps or matters of detail inevitably involve something close to second stage discussion or even negotiation.

76 Good practice dictates that, after receipt of single-stage or competitive dialogue tenders, any changes affecting price and/or design must be issued to all tenderers and a second tender exercise carried out. The public sector procurement rules require re-tendering where a change in any element of the tender represents a substantial modification of the tender (subject to various de minimis thresholds, which should be considered carefully in any single case).

77 In this regard, contractual obligations may in certain circumstances arise in the private sector also. If there is any doubt as to the position in any particular case, advice should be sought.

Recommendation, award and notification to tenderers

78 After completion of the evaluation, where the lowest or best value tender is found to be free of error or if (in a private sector procurement after an Alternative 1 or Alternative 2 procedure) the tender remains the lowest or best value, it should be recommended to the Employer for acceptance or, in a two-stage tendering procedure, as a basis for naming the tenderer as preferred bidder.

79 In all cases, private and public, it is important that all tenderers should be informed immediately of the result, since that may be of great importance for their strategic planning. In private sector cases, that notification should follow the contract award or selection of the preferred bidder.

80 However, in cases where the PC Regulations apply, acceptance of the tender should not be made, and the contract should not be entered into, before the end of the ten-day 'Standstill Period' for any challenge to the award, which commences only on notification of the intended award. The Standstill Period must be 15 days where the notification is not by facsimile or email.

81 The PC Regulations require that the "Notice of decision to award a contract or conclude a framework agreement" contains specified information and is sent not only to unsuccessful tenderers but also to the other applicants who submitted a Questionnaire.[20]

82 The traditional method of post-award notification to tenderers has been to list those tendering (in alphabetical order) and have a separate list of tender prices or best value scores (in ascending order). However, the prices or scores of unsuccessful tenderers should not be attributed to individual bidders, so, in cases where there are only three tenders, each of the unsuccessful tenderers should only be given the successful tenderer's score and, in best value cases, their own score. In the public sector, price is not normally included in the award notice due to commercial sensitivity, only the pricing evaluation score percentage will be shown.

83 Contractors also need to know how they have performed against the various individual criteria, so each should on request also be supplied both with his own individual scores and the range of scores for each of the criteria.

84 With or following the notification, any confidential information and priced documents supplied in hard copy by unsuccessful tenderers should be returned to them or, if supplied electronically, should so far as practicable be made inaccessible in accordance with the relevant protocol. Information supplied by unsuccessful tenderers that is not in the public domain should not be used for any purpose by the Employer or his advisers.

---

[20] See Regulation 86 of the PC Regulations (a Contract Finders Award Notice (r108) and an OJEU Notice Award (r50) are also generally required).

Appendix A – Preliminary Enquiry

A.1 JCT Model Form of Enquiry Letter[21]

To:[22]

Dear

Date:

Project title:

Reference No:

Employer:

We are preparing a preliminary list of tenderers for the works described in the enclosed Project Information Schedule. We should be grateful if you would let us know whether you would wish to submit a tender if selected to do so.

Should you wish to be selected, please complete the enclosed pre-qualification Questionnaire and return it to us at

____ so as to arrive not later

than[23] _______________20____.

Assessment of the responses to the Questionnaire will be carried out on the basis referred to in the Information Schedule; we will promptly inform all prospective tenderers whether they have been included in the list of those invited to tender.

This is intended to be [a single-stage/two-stage/competitive dialogue] tendering procedure, conducted in a manner consistent with the JCT Tendering Practice Note (2017 edition). As mentioned in the Information Schedule it is intended that the tender process should be conducted [electronically/in hard copy]. Contract award will be on a [best value/lowest price] basis.

We expect each contractor who now indicates a wish to tender and is then invited to do so to submit a bona fide

tender open for acceptance for a period of not less than ____________ [days/months].

An indication at this stage that you do not wish to bid will not prejudice you in relation to future projects that we put out to tender. Should you indicate now that you wish to tender but subsequently find that you are unable to do so, please inform us as soon as possible.

The Employer reserves the right to postpone the intended closing date for bids and to accept any tender or no tender at all.

---

[21] The Model Forms included in Appendix A and Appendix B are designed to be used as templates for private sector tenders and to provide a useful point of reference. The forms will require adapting for use in relation to individual projects. With regard to the public sector, in view of the rules and regulations that apply to public procurement referred to in the Introduction, public sector Employers and their professional advisers will usually have developed their own forms for use in the tendering process. For this reason, the JCT has not considered it appropriate to include model forms in this Note suitable for use by the public sector.

[22] Insert name and address of Contractor.

[23] As to periods for submission of responses to Questionnaires, see the comment in this Practice Note on the Preliminary Enquiry (2nd paragraph).

All queries and other communications in connection with the tender process should be directed to

________________ at ____[24].

It is a condition of participation in the process that no participant should at any time prior to notification of the award of the contract disclose to or otherwise discuss with any other tenderer or any third party its actual or intended tender price or any approximation of it.

Yours faithfully

For and on behalf of[25]

Enclosures: Project Information Schedule and Annexe(s); Questionnaire

---

[24] Indicate if other arrangements, e.g. for inspection of documents, mid-tender interviews and site visits, etc. are to be made through any other channel.

[25] Insert name of issuer and name and position of signatory.

A.2 Project Information Schedule[21]

Note: An asterisk* indicates text that is to be deleted or amended as appropriate.

The Project

Project title:

Description of the Works:

Site location:

[site plan attached]*

Client:

Contact address for queries and communications:[26]

Contact person(s):
Address:

Tel No:
Fax No:
E-mail:

Estimated cost range: £ to £

Requirements for Contractor's design:[27]

Anticipated starting date of the works:

Anticipated duration of the works:

Access to the Project site, types and location:

Other Employer's requirements or matters affecting the order or methods of working:

Identified risk factors:*

---

[26] Indicate if other arrangements, e.g. for inspection of documents, site visits, etc. are to be made through any other channel.

[27] For Design and Build tenders and those involving a Contractor's Designed Portion, there should, as indicated in footnote [13], be a clear demarcation of intended design responsibility. In addition it will be necessary to provide additional information, for example on site considerations, planning requirements and any proposed novation of agreements with the professional team. An outline indication should also be given of the extent of design information, etc. likely to be required with tender proposals and any applicable BIM requirements.

Consultants

Names and Addresses of Consultants:

Tel No:
Fax No:
E-mail:

Tel No:
Fax No:
E-mail:

Tel No:
Fax No:
E-mail:

Tel No:
Fax No:
E-mail:

Principal Designer for the purposes of the CDM Regulations:

Tel No:
Fax No:
E-mail:

Principal Contractor for the purposes of the CDM Regulations:

Tel No:
Fax No:
E-mail:

Tendering Procedure

Type of procedure:

Method of submitting documents (electronic/hard copy):

Closing Date for return of questionnaires:

Dates for preliminary interviews, where required:

Basis and criteria of pre-selection of tenderers:

Intended date of issue of tender documents:

Proposed Tender period: weeks

Proposed number of tenderers:

Requirements for alternative tenders and their intended basis:*

The Contract

Form of Contract:[28]

---

[28] Specify the Contract to be used and its edition/revision. State also if any Amendment and/or Supplement (e.g. for Northern Ireland, the NI Adaptation Schedule) is to apply. (If in a two-stage procedure the successful tenderer will be required in the interim to enter into a JCT Pre-Construction Services Agreement (PCSA) or similar arrangement, that also should be mentioned.)

The Contract Particulars or equivalent items for insertion in the Form of Contract[, so far as completed,]* are set out in Annex [ ]* to this Schedule.[29]

Amendments or modifications to the Contract are set out in Annex [ ]* to this Schedule

Particulars of any Listed or Named Specialists and work intended to be the subject of such sub-contracts:

Details of any required parent company guarantee and/or bonding arrangements (see Annex [ ]* to this Schedule):

Mode of execution: as a deed/as a simple contract*[30]

Tender Assessment and award

Tenders will be assessed on the basis of lowest price/best value*

The criteria for assessing best value are:[31]*

Price

[List other criteria][31]

Examination and correction of priced bills: Alternative1/Alternative2* will apply.

Date: _______________________ 20_______

---

[29] In addition to the general particulars in the Contract Particulars, the requirements for collateral warranties/third party rights as set out in the relevant Rights Particulars should also be detailed.

[30] Not applicable in Scotland.

[31] If established, specify the criteria for the tender, together with their respective weightings relative to price or their order of importance. If not established, it is sufficient to include them in the Invitation to Tender. Examples of non price criteria and sub-criteria include:

Approach
- understanding of the requirements
- initiative and team working skills
- method statement and programme
- time requirements (mobilisation period/construction period)

Design proposals
- aesthetics
- functional requirements
- life cycle costs
- flexibility in use
- maintainability

Human Resources
- project management experience and skills
- calibre of designated team
- calibre of management and support staff
- staff training and development

Technical Capabilities
- record on recent projects
- design capabilities
- BIM experience
- quality inspection capabilities
- facilities

Management procedures
- health and safety
- quality assurance systems
- risk management skills

Sub-Contractors and Supply Chain
- selection procedures and quality
- supply chain management
- length of relationships

Sustainability
- environmental policy and record
- proposals for minimising environmental impact
- proposals for systems, materials, etc.

External relations and community benefit
- community engagement
- job opportunities and training

A.3 Questionnaire[21]

(This checklist can and should be adapted as necessary, both in terms of format of the questions and the information required regarding contractors' records and capabilities. To the extent appropriate, there should be no requirement for individual prospective contractors to duplicate details covered by their industry standard accreditations. Questionnaires should also avoid details that are unlikely to be evaluated properly at the preliminary stage and can safely be left for checking at a later stage.)

To facilitate assessment of interested Contractors' capabilities and the selection of a tender list for the Project, the Contractor is requested to provide the following information, details and confirmations:

Corporate particulars

- Full company name and registration number
- Principal place of business
- Registered office (if different)
- Contact details for enquiries
- Particulars of ultimate holding company and group structure diagram
- Availability of parent company guarantee, if required
- Relevant trade registrations
- VAT registration number

Financial standing

- Report and audited accounts for last [2/3] financial years
- Statements of turnover for that period in respect of the divisional activities most closely related to the Project
- Contact details for bank references
- Alternative demonstration of financial status (where necessary for a true and fair view)

Technical capability and record

- Recent experience and record on comparable projects and in closely related fields, including (if relevant) team-working and partnering
- Contact details for referees in relation to those projects
- Particular technical skills and capabilities applicable to the Project, including design capabilities (where relevant), facilities, site management, BIM (where required) and quality assurance
- Details of current and anticipated workload and capacity

Management and Personnel

- The Company's management structure and personnel resources and the manner in which they contribute to projects of this type
- The proposed management team for this Project (including names, positions, qualifications, experience and intended roles)
- The Company's policies, procedures, arrangements for ensuring implementation and record in relation to:
    - general training and staff development
    - health and safety matters (including accident rates and safe working/preventive measures, CDM compliance, workforce information and training, occupational health and welfare)

- environmental management, including operational environmental impact and sustainable construction and operation
- quality management
- equal opportunities and diversity
- community relations and, in public procurement, local economic impact

Insurances

- Details of existing public and employer's liability cover, works insurance, product liability cover and (in cases involving design and/or professional services) professional indemnity insurance (including deductibles/excesses and renewal dates)
- Availability of additional cover specified for particular aspects of the project
- Contact details for contractor's insurance brokers

Sub-Contractors and Supply Chain

- Preliminary plans for sub-contracting and list of preferred sub-contractors
- Selection and quality assurance procedures
- Other supply chain management procedures
- Relationships with major specialists and suppliers

Good standing, material litigation, etc.

- Confirmation that neither the company nor (to the best of its knowledge) any of its past or present directors, officers or persons controlling it or acting as its agent have been charged with or convicted of any offence involving corruption, bribery, fraud, fraudulent trading, theft, money laundering or conspiracy
- Confirmation that there are no material litigation or other proceedings pending or threatened in relation to the conduct of the company's business or arising out of any projects undertaken by the company that involve or may involve the company or which it is aware involves or may involve any member of its supply chain
- Confirmation that there have in the last [3] years been no known breaches of health and safety, CDM, environmental or other statutory regulations relating to its construction activities that have led or may lead to the prosecution of or an order against the company or any of its directors, officers or other employees, or
- if any such confirmation cannot be given, to give brief particulars of the proceedings or matters in question

Appendix B – Tender Documents

B.1 JCT Model Form of Invitation to Tender[21]

Note: An asterisk* indicates text that is to be deleted and/or completed as appropriate.

To:

Project title: Reference No:

Location of the Works:

You are invited to provide a [tender/first-stage tender][32] for the Works as shown and described in, and on the basis of, the following documents:

- the Drawings listed in the attached schedule;
- the Specification/Work Schedules/Bills of Quantities/Approximate Quantities*;
- the Employer's Requirements*;
- the outline Construction Phase Plan;
- the following further documents*:[33]

The Works are to be carried out in accordance with the Contract and other conditions specified in the Project Information Schedule issued with our Preliminary Enquiry dated ______________ 20_____[, subject to such modifications as are mentioned in the further documents referred to above]*.

Please submit your tender on the attached Tender Form [by transmitting it in accordance with the attached instructions/sealed in the envelope provided] and endorsed with the Project title to ____ at ____ ____ so as to be received not later than ______ hours on ______________ 20_____[34]. Tenders received late will not be considered.

---

[32] The alternative reference to "first-stage" tender relates only to two-stage tender procedures. Where alternative tenders are being sought appropriate adaptations should be made.

[33] These must for example include the criteria and relative weightings that are to govern the award in best value tendering (if not set out in the original Information Schedule) and should include any revised versions of documents included with the Preliminary Enquiry, any form of parent company guarantee and/or bond required and (in Design and Build tenders) the required form of Contract Sum Analysis.

[34] In the case of electronic tendering, the relevant protocol and instructions should be attached or identified.

Your tender should be accompanied by the [following further documents, each in the format and completed in accordance with the attached instructions [and each enclosed in the separate envelope(s) provided]:]

- your priced document(s) [and completed Contract Sum Analysis]
- [your Contractor's Proposals]*
- [the design/selection and other documents specified [by the Employer's Requirements/in the note attached]]*

All queries and other communications in connection with the tender process should be directed to

[____].[35]

Tenders will be assessed [on the basis of lowest price/against the best value criteria set out [below/in the Project Information Schedule/in the note attached], those criteria having the relative weightings there specified].[36]

You are reminded of the need for confidentiality as set out in the preliminary enquiry letter and your agreement not to divulge your actual or intended tender price or any approximation of it to any other person or body until we notify you of the contract award. At that stage we will supply a list of tenderers (in alphabetical order) which also shows separately the relevant assessed tender scores.

The tendering procedure will be conducted in accordance with the principles set out in the JCT Tendering Practice Note (2017). The Employer reserves the right to postpone the closing date for bids and to accept any tender or no tender at all. No tendering expenses will be payable.

Signed by or on behalf of

____

Signature:

____

Position:

____

Date: ______________________ 20______

[35] Indicate if other arrangements, e.g. for inspection of documents, mid-tender interviews and site visits etc. are to be made.

[36] If for best value tenders the precise criteria weightings have not been given in the Information Schedule, they must be given now.

B.2 JCT Model Form of Tender[21]

Note: An asterisk* indicates text that is to be deleted and/or completed as appropriate.

Tender for: [Project Title][37]

To: [Employer/Consultant]

From: [Contractor]

We have examined the following documents referred to in the Invitation to Tender:

- the Drawings as there listed;
- the Specification/Work Schedules/Bills of Quantities/Approximate Quantities;*
- the Employer's Requirements;
- the Contract and the related conditions and modifications;
- the outline Construction Phase Plan;
- the following further documents:

We offer to carry out the whole of the Works as described in and in accordance with the documents referred to in this Tender for the sum of £ ____________________________ (exclusive of VAT)[38]

*[within [ ] weeks from acceptance of our tender/the Date of Possession,[39] [comprising a period of:

- [ ] weeks from acceptance to the Date of Possession; and
- [ ] weeks from the Date of Possession to the Date for Completion].]

Our fully priced document(s) [and other documents required by the Invitation to Tender, namely

____

____]

---

[37] Where alternative tenders are required a separate form of tender should be used for each tender. The form of tender must indicate clearly the nature of the alternative tender.

[38] In a two-stage tendering process there may be substituted for this paragraph and the remainder of the text (apart from any parent company guarantee confirmation required) a paragraph in terms similar to the following:

"On the basis of the priced document and a first stage tender sum of £ ____________________________ (exclusive of VAT) we offer to enter into second stage negotiations [and a JCT Pre-Construction Services Agreement (PCSA) with you in the agreed form]. Subject to satisfactory completion of those negotiations[, the preparation of priced bills of quantities] and agreement of the contract sum, we confirm our willingness to execute and complete the Works in accordance with the documents and conditions referred to in this Tender."

[39] To be adjusted and completed as appropriate prior to issue to tenderers. Where the contractor can suggest an alternative period, this latter option should in such a case be the subject of a separate tender and tenderers should be supplied with a separate form for the purpose.

[is/are attached/enclosed in the separate envelope(s) provided and marked with our name]/We agree to supply our fully priced document(s) upon which the tender is based within 3 days of being required to do so.[40]

We agree that if any obvious errors in pricing or errors in arithmetic are discovered in the priced document(s) before acceptance of this offer, they shall be dealt with in accordance with the Alternative 1/Alternative 2* procedure as described in JCT Tendering Practice Note (2017).[41]

*[For the purposes of the parent company guarantee requirements [set out in the Project Information Schedule] our parent company, namely

____

(Registered No.____________) whose registered office is at_______________________________________

_________________ has confirmed its willingness to execute and deliver to you a guarantee in the form specified.]

We undertake that in the event of acceptance of this offer, we will execute a formal contract with the Employer incorporating all the terms and conditions referred to in this offer within 21 days of being required to do so.

This tender remains open for acceptance for ___________________[42] days from the last date fixed for the submission of tenders.

Signed by or on behalf of

____

Signature:

____

Position:

____

Date: ________________________ 20________

____

Note: The completed form of tender [is to be submitted by the means specified in the Invitation to tender/sealed in the envelope provided] and must be received [by _________________________________at____ ____________________] not later than ______ hours on the ______________ day of ______________________ 20________[40]

---

[40] These provisions should be conformed with the Invitation to Tender, prior to issue.

[41] Delete whichever Alternative is not applicable, prior to issue, and see the 'Assessment and award' section of the Practice Note.

[42] For straightforward, lowest price tendering in cases not involving Contractor's design, 28 days may be sufficient. For best value tenders, Design and Build and other projects involving Contractor's design and/or assessment, longer periods are required. Substantially longer periods of validity are not uncommon.